A toolbox of ideas and information for non-instructed advocacy

A voice of their own

Annie Lawton

British Library Cataloguing in Publication

A CIP record for this book is available from the Public Library

BILD Publications is the imprint of:
British Institute of Learning Disabilities
Campion House
Green Street
Kidderminster
Worcestershire DY10 1JL

Telephone: 01562 723010
Fax: 01562 723029
E-mail: enquiries@bild.org.uk

Website: www.bild.org.uk

ISBN 1 904082 98 X

Printed in the UK by Latimer Trend
& Company Ltd, Plymouth

BILD Publications are distributed by:
BookSource
32 Finlas Street
Cowlairs Estate
Glasgow G22 5DU

Telephone: 08702 402 182
Fax: 0141 557 0189

For a publications catalogue with details of all BILD books and journals telephone 01562 723010, e-mail enquiries@bild.org.uk or visit the BILD website www.bild.org.uk

The British Institute of Learning Disabilities is committed to improving the quality of life for people with a learning disability by involving them and their families in all aspects of our work, working with government and public bodies to achieve full citizenship, undertaking beneficial research and development projects and helping service providers to develop and share good practice.

Acknowledgements

A special thank you to the Advocates from Solihull Action Through Advocacy, and particularly Barbara, Stephen, Marilyn, Peter and Mary, for allowing us to use their photographs in this publication.

About this toolbox

> *'Toolboxes, if they are any good at all, are full of stuff you need, and they are organised. You can find what you want, when you want it.'*
>
> David Pitonyak

This toolbox is not a guide to advocacy in general. It is a place to come for ideas, suggestions or contact details to help you with particular problems you might come across when you are advocating for a person with high support needs. There is no one 'right' way to do this. The important thing is to collect together a number of different tools and use these in whatever combination ensures your advocacy partner has a voice, is listened to and is taken seriously by others who can bring about change.

We got the idea for this toolbox from David Pitonyak's *Toolbox for Change* (see Resources and contacts). We hope it is full of useful things for anyone advocating for a person with *high support needs*, and we have tried to organise it so it is easy to find what you want.

By *high support needs*, we mean that the person does not communicate using words, has significant barriers to communication and/or complex physical, health or emotional needs and requires lots of extra support as a result. This could include people who have a learning disability with sight or hearing difficulties or those with a mental illness or autism.

Some words are in colour. This means that there is more information throughout the text and in sections 5 and 6 at the end of the book. Here we explain things in more detail, list useful books and resources or include contact details for you to follow up.

Contents

1. Introduction

Why is advocacy necessary for people with high support needs?

In chapter 4 of *Valuing People*, the Government Learning Disability Strategy (2001), it says that people with a learning disability should have more choice and control in their lives:

> *'People with learning disabilities currently have little control over their own lives, though almost all, including the most severely disabled, are capable of making choices and expressing their views.'*

One way of having more choice and control is to be able to speak up for yourself or to have support from an advocate to do this. But the availability of advocacy support varies across the country and there are lots of gaps. In many areas, people from black and ethnic minority communities and people who do not use words to communicate seem to be missing out.

Advocacy is about enabling every person to have a voice of their own and ensuring that they are not excluded because they do not express their views in ways that people understand. This is particularly important for people with barriers to communication and high support needs – yet these are the people who often find it most difficult to get advocacy support.

In 2001, Scope, an organisation focusing on people with cerebral palsy, set up the Independent Advocacy Campaign (IAC) because they felt there was a lack of advocacy for people with physical, sensory, communication and profound multiple impairments. Their research showed that many people with high support needs would benefit from the support of an independent advocate but that there were not enough skilled advocates or sufficient funding for this to happen. Their report from this research shows clearly that people with profound and multiple impairments and barriers to communication are among those who most need advocacy support. ('Advocating for Equality') (see Resources and contacts).

The National Autistic Society's report 'Autism: Rights in Reality' (see Booklist) showed that many adults with autism had also been unable to get access to advocacy support.

In their report to the Learning Disability Task Force in June 2003, the sub-group on People with High Individual Support Needs pointed out that:

'There is a lot of concern about advocacy not being used by people with profound learning disability and other high individual support needs. This is because it takes a lot of experience and skill to be a good advocate for someone with high individual support needs.'

One of the suggestions in this report was that the Task Force should ask advocacy groups to develop their skills for working with people with high support needs. The government realised they needed to find ways of making sure people who were being left out had the chance to get independent advocacy support and this was one of the priorities for funding advocacy work in 2004/05. Groups were asked to apply for funding and to think about ways that they could develop the skills to support people from black and minority ethnic groups and those with high support needs. The British Institute of Learning Disabilities (BILD) was asked to manage this piece of work and to visit groups to look at the different ways they are supporting people. This gave us the chance to do a lot of work with advocacy groups and organisations and to look at ways of making sure more people get advocacy support. For information about the work on advocacy for people from black and minority ethnic communities, please get in touch with BILD (see Resources and contacts).

This toolbox is for anyone who wants to find out more about advocacy for people with high support needs. This means they have what are sometimes called 'profound and multiple impairments' and are likely to have both a physical and learning disability and no formal language or means of communication. This does not mean that they cannot communicate, but often the people around them find it difficult to work out how to listen to what they are saying or to get other people to accept that they have something to say. Also, people with high support needs are usually not able to ask an advocate to work on their behalf or clearly communicate what they want the advocate to do for them. This is usually referred to as non-instructed advocacy (p. 31) and presents a whole range of dilemmas that will be discussed in the different sections of this toolbox.

Questions about how advocates can work effectively on behalf of people who cannot instruct them are highlighted with the introduction of Independent Mental Capacity Advocates (p. 35) in the Mental Capacity Act 2005 (p. 42) and proposals in the draft Mental Health Bill that people detained under the Act should have the right to advocacy. These issues have been debated in a number of seminars and workshops and the June 2005 issue of *Planet Advocacy* (see Booklist) reported on these discussions and looked at the different approaches advocates can take. Advocacy is a difficult concept for many people to understand and non-instructed advocacy challenges some definitions of advocacy and questions whether it should only be available to those who can ask an advocate to represent their wishes.

Asist (Advocacy Services in Staffordshire) produced a booklet to explain advocacy to people they support and then worked with BILD to make a short, easy-to-read guide, *Advocacy*, to tell other people about advocacy (see Booklist). The guide says:

> *'Advocacy is when a person helps you to be heard.'*

This seems a good starting point for thinking about advocacy for people with barriers to communication and high support needs:

- Why is it difficult for some people to get advocacy support and make their voices heard?
- What skills do advocates need to find out what people want to say?
- How can we help make sure people are not only heard but also taken seriously?

The first section of this toolbox will look at each of these questions in turn. The other sections have information sheets including different 'tools', practical ideas and suggestions. Examples of different ways that advocates have supported their advocacy partners are there to show that there is no one right way to do this. The important thing is to find a way that works for the individual you are supporting.

Why is it difficult for some people to get advocacy support and make their voices heard?

There are all sorts of reasons why people with high support needs miss out on advocacy support:

- Advocacy is often concerned with helping people to get the services they want. But if we are unable to find out about a person's values or wishes, how do we know if they are happy or unhappy with the support they are receiving?

- One of the key advocacy principles (p. 37) is that the advocate represents a person's interests as if they were their own, and does not make judgements about what is in the person's 'best interests'. However, advocacy with people with high support needs is often a guessing game where the advocate tries to discover what the person's own preferences might be. This can mean spending a very long time building a relationship with the person to get a picture of what is and is not important to them.

The report to the Task Force in 2003 said:

> *'Lots of people with profound learning disability find it hard to play an active role in making decisions about their lives. If someone is unable to make a decision, other people will have to make a decision that is right for that person. We need to find the best way of doing this.'*

- Advocacy for people with high support needs is sometimes referred to as 'best interest' advocacy but can give the impression that the advocate is making a decision *on behalf* of their advocacy partner rather than involving them in the decision-making process. Good advocacy support for someone with high support needs involves getting to know the person and being able to suggest what might be in *their own* interests. Because this is often based on observation and knowing the person rather than being told by them what is important, the term non-instructed advocacy (p. 31) is often used. Some people argue that this cannot be true advocacy as the person has not asked for this support and this might be one reason for people with high support needs missing out.

- Because there is a lack of skilled advocacy to enable people with high support needs to make decisions, they are vulnerable to having things decided for them.
- Suggesting or guessing what might be in the person's interests can mean that other people's values come into play. Simon Stevens suggests that the principles of 'normalisation' can mean that:

> *'All young men with profound impairments are treated like white, non-disabled heterosexual teenagers or students regardless of age or cultural reference.'*

This makes it easy to forget that the person is an individual with their own identity who might be gay, vegetarian or have a particular set of beliefs.

It is really important to see the world from the person's perspective and realise that how they understand and interpret things can affect the choices they make as the following example illustrates.

> Jonathan will ask to go shopping. He enjoys going to a particular shopping centre where he spends time sitting below a stained glass dome watching the light patterns through his fingers. He doesn't enjoy shopping and can get very upset in crowded places, but people who know him well understand what he means when he chooses to go 'shopping'. Other people might assume that he is happy to go to any shops or wants to go to buy things.

- Definitions of advocacy often use the word 'speak' and imply that the person is able to indicate clear choices, even if they need the support of an advocate to convey these to other people. But, in reality, advocacy with people with high individual support needs is much more complex than this and many people lack the skills or creativity to find different approaches to supporting your own communication (p. 53) and ways of 'listening' to what the person has to say. This can include understanding about non-verbal communication (p. 51) and how communication skills develop (p. 47).
- Sometimes people only see the person's behaviour or support needs and don't think that they could have a voice – much less anything important to say.
- People need to know about advocacy before they can get advocacy support. It isn't enough to just put information about services into 'accessible' formats. People with high support needs may depend on other people to read the information, understand what it means and decide that the person could benefit from it. If their supporters or family don't understand about advocacy then the person could miss out.
- Advocacy, particularly for people with high support needs, often gets left out of local plans so there are no resources set aside or volunteers trained with the skills they need. The Valuing People Support Team produced a toolkit to help learning disability partnership boards involve people with high support needs and another to help them plan for advocacy (see Resources and contacts).

- People with high support needs often have very limited opportunities to express preferences or choices. Their world might be very small, limited by people's attitudes and the services they use and with few opportunities to participate in their local community. Local plans, partnership boards and advocacy services who have to prioritise because of limited resources might all be focusing on issues such as people's rights, access to supported living, education or employment. While it is important that the person's rights should be protected, these issues might be too 'large' and abstract for someone with high support needs. The issue for them might be about being heard when they express a preference for being fed or bathed in a particular way or listened to when they express displeasure with an activity or situation. These choices are the building blocks upon which much more complex decisions are based and it is important that people are not excluded from advocacy because we do not acknowledge how important these everyday choices are.

What skills do advocates need to find out what people want to say?

Probably the greatest barrier to advocacy with people who have high support needs is the fact that people do not understand what they are trying to communicate. This is a two-way process, often complicated by the fact that the person might find it difficult to grasp concepts or make choices about abstract ideas and other people do not understand their wishes or preferences.

All advocates, but particularly volunteers, can often feel inexperienced in this situation. They might need more knowledge about supporting your own communication (p. 53) in order to build up a picture of their advocacy partner's total communication (p. 61). The process of building a relationship with an advocacy partner who does not respond or use formal means of communication can be very difficult and can take many months of visiting with no idea of what to 'do'.

The key is to spend time getting to know the person (p. 64), understanding their likes and dislikes and feeling confident to represent these to others. To do this, the advocate will need a whole range of skills and, perhaps most importantly, a commitment to spend time with their partner, rather than feel they have to immediately rush into action and demonstrate that they are 'doing something'.

Spending time with someone who does not seem to acknowledge their presence or respond to their attempts to communicate can be very uncomfortable for an advocate who may feel their visits are achieving very little. Spending time collecting information for a life story book (p. 65) or some other way of getting to know the person (p. 64) can feel much more constructive and also model different approaches to the person. The fact that the advocate is spending time finding out about the person, their family history, likes and dislikes and the things that are important to them can show others that the person is valued and has a contribution to make. The way that advocates develop their relationship with people who have high support needs is an important step in changing the way others see them and helps move attitudes away from care to support (see The role of the advocate, p. 26).

An advocate is supporting Ahmed who is part of a group of ten people who will be moving out from a hostel that will be closing soon. The advocate has been asked to find out what is important to Ahmed, what kind of house or flat he might like to live in and if there is anyone he might like to live with. Ahmed uses no formal communication and tends not to interact with staff or his family except to lead them to the door when he wants to go outside and has been labelled very challenging. The advocate visits weekly and sits quietly observing what is happening. After several weeks there is a meeting to discuss what is happening about the move and the manager of the advocacy service receives a phone call from Ahmed's key worker who apologises for assuming that the advocate was doing nothing. 'He sat there every week, eating our biscuits and drinking our tea and then went home after an hour or so. We thought he was doing nothing but he has gained a really accurate picture of Ahmed, the things that are important to him, the people he likes to be around and those who irritate him. We can use all this to help plan where he moves to now, and to check out if he is happy with things.'

Although it is important that advocates involve their advocacy partner as much as possible, it is also possible to get to know someone quite well without having a conversation with them. Observation is an important tool for advocates and helps you get to know the person and work out what is important to them. It will take time to establish ways of supporting your own communication (p. 53) with the person that are meaningful to them and become confident that you can represent their views or choices to others.

How can we help make sure people are not only heard but also taken seriously?

Advocacy with people with high support needs is only credible if you can demonstrate that you:

- know the person well
- understand their likes and dislikes
- can represent them without bringing in your own views or agenda

However, while people might be able to accept that an advocate can represent a person's choice between tea and coffee or different day activities within a centre, it can sometimes be difficult to convince them if the choice is more complex or controversial, for example if the person is rejecting their day service completely. This is particularly true if the advocate's interpretation of a person's views goes against service or family views or carries what others might see as an element of risk.

It could be argued that non-instructed advocacy is not valid because the person has not asked the advocate to support them or told them how to represent their wishes. However, the alternative is for that person to have no voice and to continue to be excluded from choices and decision-making.

In these situations, the advocate must clearly demonstrate a neutral view and can do this by arguing that, whatever their disability, the person has the right to be safe, comfortable and have the best quality of life possible. Rights based advocacy (p. 33) can provide a good starting point while the advocate builds a more in-depth picture of the person's likes and dislikes or in situations where there is no time to do this. It is also useful to think about what makes life worthwhile for the person, what they would describe as their perfect day or refer to agreed outcomes such as those used in Quality Network (p. 76) reviews (see Resources and contacts) which take a person-centred approach and reviews services from the perspective of the people who use them. Team members are each matched with a person using the service and find out whether ten outcomes are happening for them. Similarly, Watching Brief (p. 76) has been developed by Asist (see Resources and contacts) to provide a framework for advocates to raise questions on behalf of their partners. All these tools are discussed in more detail in What makes life worthwhile? (p. 75).

The Green Paper on adult social care – *Independence, Well-being and Choice* (p. 39) acknowledges the importance of giving people more control through individualised budgets and a choice of services. 'In Control' (see Resources and contacts) is a national programme to change the way that social care is organised. The initial programme is working with 90 people in six different areas. If people with complex needs are to have the same opportunities as everyone else to choose the services they use, those who are supporting them will need to understand capacity and consent (p. 74) and the process of supported decision-making (p. 73). This means that a person's everyday preferences can be used to help decide what their choice might be when it comes to larger or more complex decisions.

Suzanne has profound physical and sensory impairments and a life-limiting medical condition that means her health is deteriorating quite rapidly. She will be leaving residential school in the summer term and the social worker and her parents cannot agree on where she should go next. An advocate is asked to work with Suzanne and is initially given two weeks before there is a meeting to discuss what happens. The advocate begins by challenging the deadline and saying that she will need at least two months to visit Suzanne and start to get to know her. The social worker agrees to delay the meeting and the advocate visits Suzanne at least once a week at the school. She spends time observing what is happening, talking to a whole range of people who have known her for over ten years and starts to build a picture of how to tell whether Suzanne is happy or not. The advocate discovers that Suzanne does not like noisy places or people who push past her but will turn her head towards things that interest her and will become very relaxed if someone holds her hand gently or spends time close to her. She enjoys classical music, gentle massage and sessions in the sensory room and spa bath. When she is upset, her whole body becomes tense and rigid and she shakes her head violently. The advocate then visits Suzanne when she spends time at the places that are being considered for her and is able to argue that she is clearly distressed in one and much more relaxed and at ease in the other.

In these situations it is really important to collect evidence (p. 66) to support ideas about what the person may or may not want. In many cases the advocate may be pulling together what other people are already saying (for example, Suzanne's parents were very definite that she needed to live with older, quieter people). However, these messages only really become powerful when they are backed up with records of actual instances that show how this has been found out, for example life story work, photographs or a person-centred plan.

2. Advocacy

What is advocacy?

> *'Advocacy is when a person helps you to be heard.'*
>
> Asist

An advocate speaks up for someone or supports them to speak up for themselves (using whatever methods are needed to ensure the person has a 'voice' in the process).

What an advocate does:

- makes sure people are not just heard but answered
- empowers the person and promotes positive images
- works to make things happen and change
- supports the person to make choices and take more control
- works for equal rights and inclusion

What an advocate does NOT do:

- give advice
- take control away from the person
- referee an argument or dispute
- take on the role of a social worker
- make up for gaps in services that should be provided

The role of the advocate

Advocacy should never become either a crutch for the person (leading them and others to believe they will always need someone else to speak up for them) or an excuse for people to listen to or focus on the advocate rather than the person they are supporting.

Advocates model a good support relationship with their advocacy partner and demonstrate to others that the person is valued. It is particularly important that people with high support needs are seen as being supported to access a whole range of opportunities, rather than being powerless and in need of care. The relationship should present a positive image of the advocacy partner as someone who has equal status and the right to be listened to and heard, not someone dependent on the advocate in order to have a voice. Advocacy should be working towards opportunities for the person to self-advocate and situations where those around the person have developed sufficient understanding to listen to what is being communicated and act on this (see Different types of advocacy, p. 29).

It is very easy for an advocate to subconsciously convey negative messages about their advocacy partner, for example by standing to talk to someone while they remain seated, by replying to a question without giving them time to answer or by offering very obvious support or support where none is needed.

Images can be used to demonstrate the way the advocacy relationship can encourage others to see the person in a more positive light.

Advocacy – moving from care to support

With thanks to Andy Bradley, Frameworks 4 Change

Being cared for >>>>>>>>>>> **Being supported**

Routines >>>>>>>>>>>>>>>> New opportunities
Safety >>>>>>>>>>>>>>>>>> Person listened to
Basic needs >>>>>>>>>>>>>> Notice detail
Labels stick >>>>>>>>>>>>>> Equal relationships
Limiting beliefs >>>>>>>>>>>> Actively supported
Low expectations >>>>>>>>>>> Learns new skills
Lack of participation >>>>>>>> Contribution valued
Lack of options >>>>>>>>>>>> Range of options
Powerless in relationships >>>> Rights respected

The role of the advocate – key points

It is really important that the advocacy partner, staff, family and others are all really clear about the role of the advocate. It is the responsibility of the advocate themselves and their supporting organisation to explain and reinforce this.

- An advocate's first loyalty is to the advocacy partner and they should approach any situation or discussion from the advocacy partner's perspective.
- Advocates should be independent from those who provide services to their advocacy partner and who they might need to challenge. They should not be in a position where there is a conflict between their role as an advocate and anything else they do.
- Advocates cannot give advice or information but can support their partner in getting this from someone else.
- Advocacy is not befriending but friendships will often arise naturally from citizen advocacy relationships.
- Advocates do not express their own opinions but always work to find out what their advocacy partner's wishes might be. Where these cannot be clearly identified, the advocate draws on information and insight gained through their relationship with the person to suggest what they might want.
- When this is the case and they are speaking for the person, advocates should be very clear about the fact that this is not something the person has actually said but an informed guess based on their knowledge. Suggestions should be tested and reviewed.

- An advocate should always respect their advocacy partner's right to confidentiality and work within the confidentiality policy of their supporting organisation or agency.
- Advocates should be vigilant and alert their supporting organisation or other staff if they feel that their advocacy partner is at risk in any way.
- Advocates enable their advocacy partners to express their views, wishes and choices and might use any number of different strategies and tools to find out what is important to the person and what they might want to say. Through this, they support the person, safeguard their interests and pursue their goals.

Different types of advocacy

Whatever form advocacy takes, the person is always at the centre and the aim is always to find out what that person wants, how best to get this across to people who need to know, and how to bring about change.

- Self-advocacy – speaking up for yourself
- Peer advocacy – speaking up for someone with similar experiences
- Paid or professional advocacy – independent; crisis, case or issues based; time-limited
- Citizen advocacy – partnership involving an independent volunteer

There is no one right kind of advocacy. Different people need different types of support at different times in their lives. When a person is speaking up for themselves in one area of life, this doesn't necessarily mean that this will be happening all the time. For example, someone might be able to self-advocate when choosing between two T-shirts in a shop but might need support from an advocate to be involved in more abstract choices about healthcare or changes to their housing or support.

In writing about 'supported self-advocacy', Jo Clifton of VIA and John Ladle of Acting Up (see Resources and contacts) describe self-advocacy as 'a journey, but not one with a definite end or path'. They believe the different stages along the way include:

- self-awareness *'Mmm, I smell coffee.'*
- self-representation *'I like coffee.'*
- self-advocacy *'I want coffee, but people only offer me tea, I want to change that.'*

The role of the advocate is to support their advocacy partner to move from self-awareness to self-advocacy and, by doing this, bring about changes in the way the person is viewed by others and the control they have over all areas of their life.

Non-instructed advocacy

Non-instructed advocacy is based on getting to know the person and suggesting what their choices might be, rather than being asked by them for support or told how they want to be represented. The different forms this might take are discussed in articles by Joel Rasbash (PoHwer advocacy) and Chris George in the June 2005 issue of *Planet Advocacy* (see Booklist and Resources and contacts).

Advocates should always begin by assuming that the person can communicate their wishes. They should then do everything they possibly can to enable the person to understand and support them to communicate what they think. If, having done this, they are not able to find out what the person wants there are a number of approaches open to them:

- do nothing
- best interests
- rights-based
- person-centred

In practice, advocates will often use a combination of these approaches when working with people with high support needs, for example looking at the person's rights or interests in the short term but spending time getting to know them and using person-centred approaches over the longer term to check whether decisions made are in line with the person's hopes and dreams or the way they experience the world. Non-instructed advocacy should take its lead from the person and be based around their actions and reactions.

It is important for advocates and advocacy services to be very clear which approach they are adopting and any limitations it may have. Discussing each of these approaches in turn highlights the reasons why there is really no agreement about non-instructed advocacy and the need for advocacy services to have protocols to clarify the role of the advocate and explain the methods they are using.

Do nothing approach

The decision to do nothing is based on the argument that advocacy is all about representing a person's wishes, not making decisions on their behalf. If the person's wishes are unclear, is it the role of the advocate to find out what those wishes are and would it be patronising for them to assume they know what the person wants? There is already a lot of confusion about what is and is not advocacy. Does this type of advocacy confuse things still further?

On the other hand, many advocates know that, in reality, a large part of their role involves finding out what a person wants to say. Many advocates have developed skills to do this in ways that promote the person's rights and encourage others to take time to try to find out what they have to say. If advocates do nothing and do not work with people who could not instruct, would this mean that people who are often most in need of advocacy would miss out?

Best interests approach

This involves the advocate looking at all the available information, including any risks involved, and then making a judgement about which course of action is best for the well-being of the person. The approach is in line with current legislation in the Mental Capacity

Act 2005 (p. 42) where advocates are seen as informing the decision-making process, rather than making decisions on a person's behalf. Best interest advocacy is not just based on what the person is expressing (or the way that different people might interpret this) but also on thinking about what really matters for the person. Ideally, everyone should be trying to understand what the person might be communicating and thinking about ways of supporting them to do this. They should be thinking about how to give the person as much involvement as possible in the process of making the decision and thinking about their feelings, beliefs, wishes and what they might do if they were able to weigh up all the different options. The process should also involve as many different people as possible, with the advocate being valued as someone independent from the decision-making process.

But is this advocacy or just something that should be good practice in all services for people with high support needs? Does talking about a person's 'best interests' suggest that they have no role to play in the decision-making process? Does it link back to the medical approach to disability, which sees people as dependent, and leave them vulnerable to having things decided for them? Does good advocacy support mean getting to know the person and suggesting what might be in *their own interests* rather than giving the impression that the advocate is able to make a decision on the person's behalf?

Rights-based approach

A (human) rights-based approach enables an advocate to think about key issues and is particularly useful in situations where they are expected to act quickly with little time to get to know the person.

The advocate focuses on legal and moral rights, many of which are set out in law, for example in the Human Rights Act 1998 (p. 40). This approach also involves thinking about the responsibilities that other people and services have towards the person and whether they are being treated fairly and without discrimination. The advocate will go to meetings on the person's behalf and look at any proposed decisions to make sure that:

- all options have been considered
- where a person's own preferences and dislikes can be identified, these are taken into account
- no particular agendas are being pursued
- the person's civil, human and welfare rights are being respected

Looking at rights can provide a good way for an advocate to identify issues that might need to be addressed and provides a way of safeguarding the person and holding systems or services to account. It can also be useful in situations where the person appears to be rejecting the advocate's presence or where it is not possible for the advocate to spend time with them, for example because of their physical or mental health. However, sometimes a person's rights are unclear or one legal right might conflict with another. There is also a danger that, by focusing too much on rights, the advocate might miss out on the opportunity to find out about the person and ensure other people see them as unique.

Person-centred approach

This approach acknowledges that, although the person may not have a formal means of communication, they still have ways of expressing their feelings which can contribute to decision-making. Like any other person-centred approach, this involves spending time with the person, getting to know them, finding out what life is like for them, what is important to them and what their hopes and dreams might be. It looks at ways to find out what they are communicating and how we can support them to tell people what is important to them. Working in a person-centred way needs patience and a lot of time and means trying to involve as many other people as possible who know and care about the person.

However, given the shortage of advocacy support across the country, many advocates are only introduced to an advocacy partner in a crisis situation when there is not enough time to work in this way. The advocate then has to question whether spending time getting to know the person is an unacceptable delay or impractical in a given situation. Are there situations where it is acceptable to try to bring about change first and get to know the person later?

Independent mental capacity advocacy

The Mental Capacity Act 2005 (p. 42) sets out a framework for people who may not be able to make decisions. It says who can take decisions on their behalf, when this can happen and how it should be done. The Act sets up a new service – the Independent Mental Capacity Advocate (IMCA). Their role will be to help people who have no family or friends to support them in making important decisions involving health services or local authorities. This will include decisions about serious medical treatment, moving house or going into a hospital or care home. IMCAs will also attend care reviews where a person has been in care for some time. The Act said what the service must do but there were a number of questions about who should hold the budget, whether the service will be run by smaller organisations or by paying individual advocates and how the quality of services and support will be maintained and monitored. A consultation during the Summer of 2005 asked about:

- how the IMCA should be run
- funding – how and where money is used
- standards
- the training and skills that will be needed
- how to ensure the service is run properly

Independent mental health advocacy

The draft Mental Health Bill was published in September 2004. The Bill talks about working with people who have a mental disorder when they do not agree to having the treatment. A scrutiny committee in Parliament looked at the Bill and made comments based on what they had read and what other people told them about the draft Bill. Some changes will be made to the Bill before it becomes law as the Mental Health Act. One of the proposals in the Bill is that an independent Mental Health Advocacy Service will be set up to support people who are treated against their wishes.

The draft Mental Health Bill 2004 is available from the Department of Health (see Resources and contacts). There are a range of documents that aim to make the Bill easier to understand, including 'Explanatory Notes', an easy-to-read version, and 'Improving Mental Health Law – Towards a New Mental Health Act'.

Key advocacy principles

Advocacy is based on the belief that everyone has the right to:

- be respected and listened to
- be involved in decisions that affect their lives
- have aspirations for their future
- contribute to and participate in their communities

Advocacy also:

- safeguards people who are in situations where they are vulnerable
- speaks for and with people who are not being heard, helping them to express their views and make their own decisions

An advocate stands beside the person and focuses on seeing things from that person's perspective.

The advocate represents a person's interests as if they were their own and does not make judgements about what is in the person's 'best interests'.

In order to be completely on someone's side it is important for an advocate (paid or unpaid) to be independent. Their loyalty is to the person who needs advocacy. This cannot happen if they feel they have to be loyal to agencies providing care or other people or organisations in the person's life.

Ideally, advocacy schemes should have 'independence of mind, independence of place and independence of funding'. Independence of mind is the most important.

Good advocacy does not seek confrontation but is not afraid to challenge practice or policies if necessary.

Good advocacy schemes work hard to be respected for the quality and integrity of their work.

Advocacy in practice

Advocacy with people with high support needs who cannot instruct an advocate is very different from other types of advocacy and raises all sorts of questions. Although most people would support the principle that advocacy should be readily available to anyone, if the person cannot give the advocate permission to act, can we rely on third parties to do this? How does the advocate know when to act and how do we judge 'success' if the person is not setting and reviewing goals with their advocate? Most crucially, where is the accountability and how can the person say if they are not happy with their advocate?

Although advocacy services are usually very clear about their aims and objectives, it is sometimes difficult to set out their working practices clearly in order to answer some of these questions. For this reason we have included references to some draft documents that might help organisations shape or review their own policies.

Some draft policies can be downloaded from BILD at www.bild.org.uk or you can order copies from BILD Advocacy Services on 01562 723025.

Government policy and advocacy

There are some key pieces of recent Government policy which it is useful for advocates to know about:

1. **The Green Paper on adult social care – Independence, Well-being and Choice**

   This document recognises that people can make meaningful choices about what happens in their lives if they are supported and empowered to do this. Proposals include giving people more control over the services they use or support they receive by putting them in charge of how the money is spent. This could be done through having a direct payment to purchase these directly or through individualised budgets which would give people information about the cost of services and involve them in decisions about how money is spent on their support. Consultation on the Green Paper ended on 28 July 2005.

More information is available from www.dh.gov/socialcare or copies of publications relating to this (including easy-read versions) can be ordered from the Department of Health (see Resources and contacts).

2. The Human Rights Act

The Human Rights Act (1998) sets out the constitutional rights of all citizens – regardless of a person's race, ethnicity, religion, gender or disability.

The Act came into force in Britain in October 2000 and means that it is unlawful for any public body (or anyone working for such a body) to breach the European Convention on Human Rights unless an Act of Parliament means that they have no choice. Although it is a complex piece of legislation, written in complicated legal language, its aim is to make it easier to challenge any abuses of human rights. BILD has produced an 'easy-read' guide to the Act – *Easy Guide to the Human Rights Act 1998* – (see Booklist and Resources and contacts) which focuses on its implications for people with a learning disability.

The Act contains 'articles' and 'protocols' – statements that explain the different rights under the Act. The BILD guide discusses those that are most relevant to anyone supporting a person with a learning disability. These include:

- the right to life
- no torture, inhuman or degrading treatment
- the right to liberty and personal freedom
- the right to marry and have a family
- freedom from discrimination
- no one has the right to destroy or abuse rights

An advocate needs to encourage others to think about rights when discussing potential risks for a person they are supporting. It is very easy to focus on health and safety issues while forgetting the risks to the person's status as a citizen and full member of society and the Human Rights Act provides a framework for this approach. For example, strapping someone who is able to walk into a wheelchair, without exploring other ways to manage their behaviour and keep them safe, could be challenged under Article 3 (no torture, inhuman or degrading treatment).

Obviously, it is best to try to resolve problems locally by talking to key workers, social workers, doctors or other professionals, as challenges under the Act can be complicated and time-consuming. However, the framework does suggest areas to consider and national organisations such as the Department for Constitutional Affairs Human Rights Team or Disability Rights Commission can offer advice and support (see Resources and contacts).

3. The Mental Capacity Act 2005

This Act, which will come into effect in 2007, was first published as the draft Mental Incapacity Bill in 2003 but was substantially revised after consultation and scrutiny by a Houses of Lords and Commons Joint Committee. The Act sets out a framework for people who may not be able to make decisions. It says who can take decisions on their behalf, when this can happen and how it should be done.

It had been clear for a long time that the law needed updating to protect vulnerable people, carers and professionals and to clarify who can take decisions in which situations and how they should go about it. This ensures that an individual who is thought to lack capacity is put at the centre of the decisions being made and remains the focus. One of the changes made to the draft Bill was the introduction of an Independent Mental Capacity Advocate (p. 35) (IMCA) Service to provide special safeguards for people who lack capacity to make serious decisions. There are some similarities between this and the role of the non-instructed advocate.

The Act provides a framework for supporting anyone over 16 years old who is thought to lack the capacity to act or make a particular decision for themselves. The decision may be about day-to-day matters or major life-changing events. It sets out rules for making decisions on another person's behalf and sets up a process for resolving any disputes or difficulties. Some of the framework already exists in common law but the Bill also builds on good practice developed in recent years.

The Act will:

- provide a Code of Practice giving guidance on working and dealing with people who are thought to lack capacity
- provide a checklist to work through when deciding what is in a person's best interests
- provide for 'general authority' which will allow a person to act on behalf of another – a person acting under the 'general authority' does not have a new authority to intervene in the life of someone who lacks capacity, but this could protect carers from liability when they act in the best interests of a person who cannot consent
- provide for lasting powers of attorney (LPAs) which will allow people to appoint an attorney to act on their behalf if they should lose capacity in the future
- create a system of court appointed deputies to replace and extend the current system of receivership in the Court of Protection
- provide for advance decisions to allow people to make a decision to refuse treatment if they should lose capacity in the future – the Act sets out the circumstances in which advance decisions may be followed by doctors together with safeguards that will seek to ensure that the person making them is fully informed and that they have not changed over time
- introduce a new criminal offence of neglect or ill treatment that can be used against anyone who has ill-treated or wilfully neglected a person who lacks capacity

- will establish a new Court of Protection to consider applications for financial decisions in serious healthcare cases which are currently dealt with by the High Court. The practical working of the court will be designed around the needs of the person lacking capacity
- establish the Public Guardian as the registering authority for Lasting Powers of Attorney and superviser of their activities

The Act does not change the law on euthanasia or on withdrawal of artificial nutrition and hydration.

The Mental Capacity Act establishes a new statutory scheme known as the Independent Mental Capacity Advocate (p. 35) (IMCA) service to provide additional safeguards for certain people who are seen as vulnerable and who lack capacity to take decisions. This service will be available for people who have no close relatives, friends or other person to help protect their interests. The independence of the IMCA is stressed, as is their duty to advise in the best interest of the vulnerable person that they are supporting.

The Act and accompanying papers can be found at:
www.dca.gov.uk/menincap

4. The Mental Health Bill

The Bill was formally announced in the Queen's Speech in May 2005. It will be debated by Parliament before November 2006.

The Mental Health Alliance is a group of organisations working to ensure that the new Bill will improve the lives of people with mental health needs (including people with a learning disability and additional mental health needs).

Find out more at www.mentalhealthalliance.org.uk

5. Disability Discrimination Act 2005

The Disability Discrimination Act 2005 updates the Disability Discrimination Act of 1995. It introduces a new responsibility for all public services to consider disabled people in everything they do. It creates new rights for disabled people concerning the use of public transport and for disabled tenants to make reasonable adjustments to their homes.

For more information go to www.drc.org.uk

6. Equal treatment: closing the gap

The Disability Rights Commission (DRC) is looking at why people with mental health needs and people with learning disabilities get ill more often than other people.

To find out more, go to www.drc.org.uk

3. Communication

How communication skills develop

Thinking about how we learn to communicate can help an advocate to understand what their partner might be saying or how to support their communication.

When we are first born we smile or cry just because of the way we are feeling. This is a reflex response to a situation and, because we are not trying to communicate with anyone, is called pre-intentional behaviour or communication. However, people will often act as if we are trying to tell them something and will guess what might be making us happy or sad. Their response to our behaviour or communication helps us learn that by doing different things we can make people act in certain ways and use this to get what we want. When we do something on purpose to get a reaction it is called intentional behaviour or communication.

How intentional behaviour helps us learn to communicate
When John is in the canteen, he tends to stiffen and twitch every time someone shouts or clatters a plate. His key worker might guess from

John's jumping movements that he doesn't like the noisy canteen and decide to help him move somewhere quiet to eat his lunch. If John learns to associate his movements with her response, he might start to control these to tell people he wants to be moved away from something he doesn't like. Over time, this could develop into an individual sign or gesture that John can use to show he is unhappy or uncomfortable.

Advocates might learn to understand how a person feels from their:

- cries or other sounds
- looks
- smiles
- voice changes
- body movements or position

The advocate observes what is happening for a while and then responds to what they think the person might be telling them.

When that person realises that someone is taking notice they might start to:

- reach or move towards objects
- use different sounds
- focus on an object or person
- push away things they don't want

When someone learns to control their behaviour to tell people what they want, it is important to make sure everyone knows what the person is trying to tell them. It is important to talk to other people who know the person well to find out how they understand their communication. It may be that your first guess about what the person is trying to tell you is wrong and needs to be reviewed, but this is easier to do if everyone is working in the same way and sharing their understanding of the person's communication.

A positive and consistent response from everyone will encourage the person to develop this communication while mixed messages or negative responses can result in them 'switching off' to the process. However, it can sometimes be very difficult to identify communication if the behaviour is offensive. For example, if a person is spitting at particular staff who help with personal care, this can result in an emotive situation where it is not easy to consider that this may be a way of indicating that he prefers a particular person or way of working. If an advocate receives this kind of treatment, they will need good support and supervision to be able to stand back and consider what the person might be trying to say and not interpret the action as a personal affront. In the same way, it might be difficult for an advocate to convince staff that when a person rams certain people in the shins with her wheelchair, it could be a response to them entering her room without knocking, rather than a deliberate physical assault. If the purpose of communication is to let people know what you think and achieve a reaction, then people will quickly learn the best way to achieve this.

Having suggested what a person might be trying to communicate, it is essential to work with a consistent response in order to test this out. Communication passports, personal dictionaries or talking photograph albums are some examples of tools to support your advocacy partner's communication (p. 57) which can help people interpret what the person is saying in the same way. It is also important to review your understanding of a person's communication regularly to take account of any changes in the way they convey different meanings or choices or any new suggestions of what they might be trying to say.

Non-verbal communication

> *'No matter how hard one may try, one cannot* not *communicate. Activity or inactivity, words or silence – all have message value.'*
>
> Donnellan et al 1984

Working with an advocacy partner who doesn't use words to communicate can seem a daunting task, but the diagram above right shows just how little communication is through the words and how much meaning is conveyed in other ways.

Understanding that facial expression, body language or tone of voice carry far more meaning than the actual words we use, can help an advocate look for other ways of finding out what their advocacy partner might be saying and also ensure that they are aware of any mixed messages their own posture or voice might be giving.

How we communicate

- words/phrases

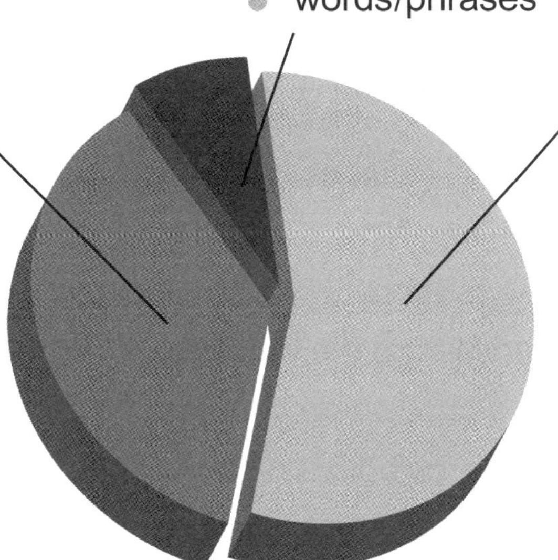

37% How we sound

- rate
- volume
- stress/ intonation
- pitch
- fluency

55% Things we see

- facial expression
- gaze pattern
- head movements
- hand/arm/leg movements
- body positioning

Interpreting non-verbal communication

It is really important that advocates take time getting to know their advocacy partner and learning the meaning of different types of non-verbal communication. Does James's gaze move towards things he is interested in, or the sounds he makes increase in volume and frequency when he is excited and pleased? It is important not to make assumptions that these communications are as they might appear. For example, Abdul's smile might be an effort to attract attention when he is bored, while his loud cries might be a sign that he is feeling very happy. If people agree a meaning for his non-verbal communication and respond to it in the same way, Abdul is encouraged to use this as a way of telling people what he wants. Sometimes communication may take the form of behaviour that is challenging or offensive and it is important to take time to try to identify what the person might be trying to say.

A communication passport (p. 59) or personal dictionary (p. 59) is a good way of supporting people who do not use words and who might find it difficult to understand complex language (see Tools to support your advocacy partner's communication, p. 57).

Checking your own non-verbal communication

If you put your hands on your hips, a scowl on your face and shout 'I really like you' at someone they will probably think you mean the exact opposite. Your body language and tone of voice will have a far greater impact than the actual words you use. Advocates must be really careful that their non-verbal communication matches the words they use. Their advocacy partner may gain meaning from their tone of voice, gestures or single words, even if they do not understand everything that is said. Gestures or more formalised signing can be an excellent way to get across emotions or other things that are difficult to convey in words (see Why sign and speak? (p. 55) in Supporting your own communication, p. 53). Sending out 'mixed messages', either subconsciously or by using sarcasm or some types of humour, can confuse people who may find it difficult to interpret the subtleties of this type of communication. It is also important to think about whether the person has good vision and hearing – if there is any type of sensory impairment, this could mean they are missing out on a lot of your communication.

Supporting your own communication

An advocate needs as much information as possible about how their advocacy partner communicates and the things that might affect this. A communication checklist (p. 62) is a useful tool for making sure you have thought about as many things as possible.

An advocate might be asked to give information to their advocacy partner and there are a number of things to bear in mind:

- Is the information important to the person and does it impact on their everyday life?

  For example, someone might want to know where their room is in the house, rather than all the details of their tenancy agreement.

- Be clear about why the person needs the information, how much information they need and when this should be given – too much information at the wrong time can be as ineffective as having no information.
- If the person is being given a summary, be clear about who else needs to understand the information and who will be holding the more detailed information on their behalf.

See Norah Fry guidance on information (see Resources and contacts).

There are a number of ways that you can support and clarify your communication. However, it is important to realise that there is no 'one size fits all' solution. The same person will probably need different levels or types of support depending on their mood, their health, the environment or the type of information being communicated:

- An advocate should ask a qualified speech and language therapist for advice on what communication methods to use.
- Making an attempt to try different ways to support communication can be more important than getting it right first time. The advocate and their advocacy partner will both learn together and decide what works.
- Using visual information that is too complex (pictures, symbols, written text, etc) can be confusing and make the person feel they have 'failed' to understand or communicate – keep it simple and consistent.
- Using actual objects (objects of reference) is not as cognitively demanding as symbols and they are easier to recognise.
- Sensory cues can let the person know that you are there and 'cue' them into your visit – perhaps wearing a particular perfume or aftershave, playing a particular piece of music or bringing along a particular object for them to feel or hold.
- New signs or symbols are often easier to understand if they are used in context. For example, miming raising a glass when you are in a pub and want to find out what the person wants to drink.
- Direct immediate methods such as pointing, miming or visiting actual locations are easier to understand than indirect or abstract references to things.
- People can often find it difficult to understand cause and effect or the full implications of information they are given. Try to keep information clear and factual.
- Think about social or cultural differences or influences.
- An advocate should not make assumptions about their advocacy partner – but be prepared to be surprised.

The June 2005 edition of the *British Journal of Learning Disabilities* focuses on communication and giving people information (see Booklist and Resources and contacts).

The articles are written from different perspectives but all stress the importance of remembering that communication is individual and personal and that people with a learning disability should always be involved in decisions about how information should be presented.

Why sign *and* speak?

People often only sign if other people around them are signing too.

Signing or gestures can encourage other people to communicate.

Signing is a good way to get across emotions which might be hard to explain with pictures, words or symbols.

Signing can help people understand what you are saying.

Signing can help get the person's attention, letting them know that you are talking to them. Signing may help to keep someone focused.

Tools to support your advocacy partner's communication

An advocate needs to be aware of a whole range of different tools that might support their advocacy partner's communication. As with advocacy itself, there is no right or wrong tool for the job and an advocate will probably use all sorts of different combinations in order to make sure the person is listened to and taken seriously.

Good communication depends on a whole combination of things such as health, environment, physical comfort, energy levels or mood. If a person is having a good day they may be happy to communicate, but on a bad day, may just prefer to spend time alone. If you look at the situation from the person's perspective and are guided by them as to what they see as important, there is more chance that they will want to communicate about this than if you go in with your own agenda. Having someone who is just there for them and who is working one to one can motivate some people to communicate far more than they would in a group situation.

Matching a person's communication makes them feel valued and is more likely to encourage them to use their skills than if inappropriate communication is used. Phoebe Caldwell, Melanie Nind and David Hewitt describe the use of this intensive interaction to 'get inside the world' of people with high support needs and details of their publications are included in the Booklist. Intensive interaction is a really good tool for advocates and gives them the opportunity to start a 'conversation' with someone by mirroring their actions and treating them as the building blocks of communication. For example,

Bernard rocks back in his seat and slaps his hand down on the table. The advocate mirrors this back to Bernard and continues to do this each time he does it. After a while, Bernard pauses and looks at the advocate before moving; he is checking for a reaction and a very basic communication has begun. It may take some time for the person to respond and the responses, such as a slight movement of the head, may be very small but this is still a valuable start to communication.

There is no definitive list of tools to support your advocacy partner's communication – this will always be a very personal process with people developing their own signs, gestures, sounds or other communication systems. The advocate's role is to ensure that other people recognise and value this communication and that their partner has easy access to the tools. For example, it is no use working on a communication book if only the staff at the day centre know about it and Mum and Dad, staff at the respite flat or the escort on the bus don't even know it is in the person's bag. It is worth checking regularly that everyone is using the book.

There are many ways of recording a person's communication so that other people can understand what they are saying. If you use photographs in a communication book, it is really important to remember that these are tools with a specific purpose for the person to indicate what they want – they are not photograph albums to browse through casually. The examples that follow provide ways of collecting evidence (p. 66) about the person's preferences, choices or dislikes and there is more information in the later sections.

Personal dictionaries, communication dictionaries or communication passports can consist of pictures of signs, gestures or other aspects of the person's communication with explanations of what this means. They are a way of recording how others interpret the person's communication and how the person receives or understands communication. They can ensure that the level and pace of communication is appropriate and can detail specific phrases, the rate of utterance and the tone of voice or intonation so that these are used consistently. Communication passports can also explain the best way to attract and maintain a person's attention.

Photographs are a good way of recording gestures or body language and video is also a useful tool, but less easy to use in everyday situations. Paradigm has some useful information about person-centred approaches to communication (see Resources and contacts).

Talking photograph albums (see Resources and contacts) consist of a number of double plastic pockets to hold photographs. Each page has a small button that allows a short message to be recorded and played back whenever the page is viewed and the button pressed. There are numerous ways to use these to support communication and the Liberator website (see Resources and contacts) lists many of these. They are particularly useful in situations when you want more subtle communication than just pointing to a symbol or looking at a picture. For example, someone who is fed only by tube might point to a picture of a pub or a pint of beer to indicate he wants to go out for the evening. However, the person who takes him will probably not think to buy him a pint because he can't drink it. In the talking photograph album, a photograph of the person in the pub with a pint of beer in front of him could be accompanied by a message saying 'I still enjoy going to the pub, even though I can't drink. Please buy me a pint so I don't feel left out'.

Similarly, video can convey complex information very simply. For example, one organisation produces short video clips of how tenants with very complex physical and health needs like to be lifted and moved. These are played to new or agency staff with the person present and included in discussions and can give a far better picture of what makes the person feel comfortable than written descriptions in a care plan or handover file.

Multimedia profiling (see Collecting evidence, p. 66 and Resources and contacts) pulls together photographs, sounds and video clips to explain a person's communication. At the other end of the scale, small plastic keyrings with holders for three or four passport-sized photographs can be used for someone to indicate preferences. For example, photographs of people who are important to the person and who they might want staff to contact on their behalf.

The possibilities are endless but it is important to remember that communication is a very personal skill and needs to have meaning for the individual. If someone does not relate to photographs or two-dimensional representations, a photograph album or symbol chart will have no meaning for them. They might prefer to use a swimming costume to represent swimming at the leisure centre or a knife and fork for meal times. A box containing objects related to different activities or pegs on the wall to hang up objects of reference might be far more relevant to them. Whatever method or combination of methods is used to support the person's communication, it is important to start with the basics so everyone understands how to interpret whether they are happy, sad, bored, angry, hungry, want to be on their own, etc. It is very easy to rush to record more complex communications without first checking that everyone can understand how to ensure the person is comfortable, happy and safe.

Total communication

Advocates might hear or read references to 'total communication'. This simply means communicating in any way you can – not just talking but using:

- signing
- pictures
- symbols
- photographs
- objects
- gesture
- body movement
- facial expressions
- writing
- drawing
- miming or drama
- other art forms

Total communication acknowledges that people who don't use words *can* and *do* communicate. It is simply a matter of other people being more creative and finding the tools that enable them to communicate, build relationships, let other people know what they feel or think and be included.

Communication checklist

Good communication depends on:

- how well you can hear
- how well you can see
- how comfortable you are feeling
- how alert and attentive you are
- how well you can understand what is happening
- how well you can express yourself to someone else
- how interested and motivated you are to communicate

Nicola Grove 'Communication and PCP' BILD unpublished handout, (see Resources and contacts)

As an advocate, it is important to think about:

- How you and the person are positioned. Are you both comfortable and relaxed? Can you make eye contact, see and hear each other? Is there anything physical such as hearing or sight problems, medication, pain, physical positioning or tiredness that might affect communication?

- What you know about the person that can help you understand them and that you can build on. For example, are there any Elvis CDs or family photographs on the shelf? Are they wearing a Liverpool FC T-shirt? Is there an activity you could do together that would stimulate communication?
- Whether the person can understand you. If they are finding it difficult they might be saying yes all the time, giving different answers to the same question, not responding at all or behaving in ways that can be seen as challenging.
- What it is the person understands. Is it the actual words you are using or your voice patterns, tone of voice or gestures? Can they understand single words, short sentences?
- Talking to other people and watching the person to find out how they like to communicate. For example, what personal or more formal signs, gestures or pointing to objects or people do they use? Do they use pictures, symbols or objects of reference? What do their body language, body positioning or facial expressions tell you? Do they use a communication aid or book?
- What changes you need to make to the way you communicate to match the person's communication or gain their attention?

  For example, do you need to talk clearly and slowly, use signs and gestures, point to objects and people, use your face and body language, give them time to respond?
- Whether everyone else is communicating consistently with the person. If not, what needs to happen to change this?
- Whether the person wants to spend time with you today. Or would it be better to come back another time to reinforce the fact that they have control over this communication?

It is also important to think about the environment and how it might affect the person's communication and your own:

- Noise makes it hard to hear and might make you tense or agitated.
- Somewhere too quiet might feel too formal. Could you suggest some quiet background music?
- Communal rooms that are part of someone else's home are difficult to manage. It is not so easy to suggest turning off the TV, even if you are sure no one is watching it.
- If the room is familiar to the person, check whether it has any negative or different associations. Is it where they meet their psychiatrist or where formal reviews are held?
- How is the furniture arranged? Does it feel too formal? Are the chairs comfortable?
- Big spaces can make it hard to hear and see.
- Are people going to be coming in and out all the time?
- Is there a window or things to look at to provide topics of conversation?

Getting to know the person

Getting to know the person follows on from the section Tools to support your advocacy partner's communication (p. 57) but includes other information about the person that they may not be able to give you themselves.

Life story books and person-centred planning are probably the best known tools for finding out as much as you can about a person. Life story books often include detailed personal histories while person-centred planning will also record a person's hopes and dreams (or what the person's circle of support feel these might be, based on their likes, dislikes, important people and places, etc). However, informally you can find a lot of information by observing the person and their reactions to different people, places and things, talking to as many people as possible who know them, looking at photographs, souvenirs, treasured possessions or all those battered leaflets and programmes they carry in their bag.

An advocate needs to know and understand as much as possible about their advocacy partner so that in situations where the person cannot indicate a clear preference the advocate can suggest what this might be – based on this knowledge. Where there is conflict or disagreement, it is useful to have evidence (p. 66) to back up suggestions.

When people do not use words to communicate, it is easy to focus on practical, concrete subjects and not allow people the opportunity to explore their feelings or emotions. In 1998 the From the Inside Looking Out (FILO) project set out to help people with a learning disability develop their personal literacy skills. Pilot courses have been run and a training pack is planned. FILO is based at Talkback (see Resources and contacts).

‘Emotional literacy’ enables people with a learning disability to:

- be aware of their feelings
- find ways to communicate their emotional needs to others
- respond positively and effectively when someone else expresses emotion

Collecting evidence

When an advocate is supporting someone who does not use words to communicate, there is always going to be an element of guesswork about what the person may or may not want. It is important to find ways of linking any suggestions about preferences or actions directly back to the person to make it clear that they are not based on the advocate’s own views or personal agenda. Evidence sounds a fairly formal way of describing this but what the advocate actually needs to do is collect examples of situations, events, activities or observations that show how they have reached a particular conclusion.

> Joseph is about to move into his own flat but his behaviour is becoming more and more erratic. His parents feel that this is his way of saying that he doesn’t want to move while his social worker feels things should go ahead as planned. Joseph’s advocate knows that he is very impatient about everything and that he finds it difficult to understand the concept of time. She takes Joseph to see his new flat and notices that he is very happy and excited when he arrives but very agitated when he leaves. They visit again and his reactions are the

same. His advocate feels that Joseph wants to move but finds it difficult to understand the delays. She notes his reactions and also makes a timeline with pictures to show all the things that need to happen before he can move. A photograph of Joseph is moved along the line as each thing is completed, for example, when he signs the agreement or chooses his carpets and curtains. Joseph is much calmer and his advocate feels that this, together with his reactions to the visits, is evidence that he wants to move but is unsettled by the process. She uses this to challenge his parents' suggestions and to put pressure on the social worker to update Joseph on progress and to chase the housing association for a date for him to move in.

Often a meeting is called to discuss particular issues or choices and there can be very different views about what the person might want to happen. If people are clear about the purpose of the meeting and are asked to bring along 'evidence' to support their views, this can often result in much more person-focused and positive discussion. This process can be formalised using forms to let people know what decision will be discussed and to enable them to record their thoughts and bring these to the meeting. Nicola Grove discusses this approach in more detail in *See What I Mean* (see Booklist) and there are suggestions for forms that can be used to encourage people to back up their statements about what the person's preferences might be.

Multimedia profiling is one way of bringing together video clips, photographs, written materials, music and speech. They are held on a computer and can be used to give a picture of the person's likes, dislikes, things they have done and things that interest them. The person's reactions to the various images or sounds can provide further evidence of what might be important to them. This can be a powerful tool and give the person a 'voice' and a presence at review or planning meetings. Acting Up, Mencap and HFT (see Resources and contacts) can provide more information and examples of how this can be used.

Probably one of the most powerful tools for ensuring that people realise that a particular choice or course of action is directed by the person themselves, is to refer to their person-centred plan. Challenged by Complexity was an ARC project that highlighted different approaches to person-centred planning with people who have high support needs. BILD, Paradigm, Circles Network and the Foundation for People with Learning Disabilities are some of the organisations that can also provide more information about person-centred approaches (see Resources and contacts).

Observation

If only a small percentage of our communication is based on words, it follows that an advocate can learn a lot by observing things like their advocacy partner's body language, facial expression and tone of voice. It is also important to look at the actions and responses of other people and the way they relate to the person.

Advocates often feel that they are expected to rush into action on behalf of the person, particularly if the referral relates to a crisis or a particular issue. It takes a lot of confidence to sit quietly in the corner of a lounge or day centre, watching what is happening and getting a sense of what life is like for their advocacy partner, but it can give a very clear idea of what the issues might be. It is particularly useful to do this at the beginning of an advocacy relationship, perhaps before you have even been introduced to the person, as it can provide lots of information about how the person communicates, where and when they might like to meet you and what interests them and could be used to start a 'conversation' with them.

> An advocate has been asked to work with Robert because he has started to slap certain members of staff when they go into his room. He is 50 years old and has Down syndrome and the community nurse is concerned that he may be showing early signs of confusion and dementia. The advocate visits at a busy time of day when staff are changing shifts and sits quietly in the lounge instead of visiting Robert in his room. He notices that some people knock on Robert's door or call out before they enter while others walk straight in and are greeted by a startled shout and a slap. The advocate feels there is a connection and suggests that Robert might be challenging people who do not respect his privacy by knocking or announcing themselves. The other suggestion is that Robert's sight is failing and he is frightened when people suddenly appear.

If an advocate is observing what is going on, it is important for this to be an informal, natural activity rather than one giving the impression that they are spying on other people. It is important to stress that advocates have the luxury of coming to a situation fresh and being able to stand back and look at things in a way that people living or working in a situation cannot. This must be seen as 'people watching' rather than an inspection or monitoring visit.

12
9
3
6

4. Choice and decision-making

Supporting choice

The advocate's role is not just to find out what their advocacy partner wants but also to support them in making these choices and developing these skills.

Advocates will often be supporting people who have very few positive experiences of making choices and it is important to recognise that this is a skill that needs to be practised and developed like any other.

Supporting choice-making

An advocate could help to develop choice-making skills in a number of ways:

- One of the first steps *might* involve teaching the person the mechanics of choice.
- A good way to begin is to offer a known desired item and a neutral or non-preferred item.
- It can be easier to offer choices *within* activities rather than *between* activities at first.

- If you doubt that the person understands use the simplest representation possible, for example real objects.
- If presenting a choice of two, swap around to ensure the person isn't choosing:
    - the last thing you said
    - one particular item in a visual display
- Be aware of introducing your own preference or bias by stressing a particular word, by eye-pointing, etc.
- Sometimes people find it easier to cope with choice-making when options are defined and limited. For example, instead of an open question like 'What do you want?' use a 'forced alternative' like 'Do you want fish or sausage?'
- Be aware that intentional choice-making might make things easier for you as a partner but it *can* be stressful for the person themselves.
- Sometimes the best option is to become familiar by observing how the person shows their likes and dislikes.
- Developing choice-making skills may take a long time, and many different methods may need to be explored, particularly for complex choices that are life-changing.

Choice-making and autism

A lot of assumptions are made about people with autism and their ability to make choices. It is really important to remember that autism is a complex disability that affects the way a person communicates and relates to people around them. Everyone with autism is different and the advocate will need to take time to try to understand the world as the person sees it. However, it is inevitable that there will be changes in everyone's life and good long-term support can mean that the person and their advocate are better equipped to deal with this (see National Autistic Society in Resources and contacts).

Supported decision-making

Decisions tend to be more significant and life-changing than choices. An advocate will often be asked to support someone in making a decision about where to live, financial matters or other complex or abstract ideas and the process of supported decision-making can ensure that the person has as much involvement as possible in this.

The law now recognises that people can be supported to make important decisions and that our capacity to do this can vary from time to time and between different decisions (Mental Capacity Act 2005 (p. 42)). Supported decision-making builds on those areas where the advocate knows what a person's choice might be.

> Sally has the chance of supported employment but her advocate is not sure whether she understands the idea of work or what is available to her. Sally loves to be outdoors, dislikes crowded places and noisy environments, relates better to one or two people and needs to be active. Placements are available in a supermarket, garden centre, café or small farm. Although Sally cannot make a choice between these abstract options, her advocate feels that her preference would be for the farm and suggests that Sally visits one to find out more.

Legal issues – capacity and consent

The Mental Capacity Act 2005 (p. 42) sets out a framework for people who may not be able to make decisions. It says who can take decisions on their behalf, when this can happen and how it should be done.

The key principles of the Act to bear in mind when supporting someone who might be described as 'lacking capacity' to make a particular decision are:

- **An assumption of capacity:** Everyone has capacity unless it is established that they lack it.
- **Participation in decision-making:** Everyone should be given the support they need to make their own decisions or to participate as fully as possible in decision-making. A person must not be treated as if they are unable to make decisions unless every effort has been made to support them in the decision-making process.
- **Capacity is decision specific:** Assessment of someone's capacity must be based on the actual decision to be taken at the time it needs to be taken – there should be no blanket label of incapacity.
- A person must not be treated as unable to make decisions simply because their decisions are unwise. They must retain the right to make what might be seen as **eccentric or unwise** decisions.
- **All decisions must be in the person's best interests:** Decisions should be made in their best interests, taking account of their likes and preferences.
- Decisions made on behalf of someone else should be those which are **least restrictive** of their basic rights and freedoms.

What makes life worthwhile?

> *'In an effort to provide special services to people it is easy to forget the ordinary everyday things that people need.'*
>
> David Pitonyak 'Notes for Parents'
> (see Resources and contacts)

The starting point for any advocacy relationship is to find out what is important to the advocacy partner and act upon this, but sometimes it is difficult to find out what the person might want. It may be useful to think in terms of the person's quality of life in relation to what anyone else might expect to have. A number of organisations use this as a way of encouraging people to think about what life might be like for the person and what might need to change.

In a training session, Frameworks 4 Change (see Resources and contacts) ask people to list ten things that 'make life worthwhile' for them. These are written up on a flip chart and common themes identified. In BILD advocacy training (see Resources and contacts), participants work in groups to negotiate their individual suggestions down to a list of ten themes. In both instances, the resulting lists are certain to contain references to relationships, choice, freedom and opportunities rather than tasks and services.

The Quality Network offers a person-centred way of reviewing services using ten 'outcomes' which look at what life is like for people using that service. These outcomes focus on:

- involvement in everyday choices
- important decisions
- everyday activities
- the local community
- work or valued activities
- friendships and relationships
- being respected
- being safe
- getting help to stay healthy
- the person's relationship with their family or other important people in their life

An advocate can use these or similar headings to question what is happening in their advocacy partner's life. For example, are they supported to form relationships, given choices and valued for themselves? However, it is important to remember that this is only a starting point and a framework to suggest areas to explore. Everyone is unique and individual and, although the same sorts of things might be important to most people, their priorities might be very different.

Asist (see Resources and contacts) have developed 'Watching Brief' as a way for advocates to represent a person when they cannot understand or find out what their advocacy partner might want.

It is based on 'eight domains to a quality of life', which were developed by Chris Sterling from North Staffordshire Housing Consortium and is a way of suggesting questions that the advocate might ask on behalf of their partner. For example, under the heading 'community presence' the advocate might ask what staff are doing to support the person to attend public swimming sessions or why they feel it is necessary for them to swim at a local special school rather than the leisure centre. By doing this, the advocate makes it clear that they are not expressing a view or suggesting a particular course of action.

When using 'Watching Brief' or any other tool that protects or argues for ordinary life principles, it is very important that the advocate makes it clear that they are working in this way and not expressing either their own views or the views of their advocacy partner.

5. Booklist

The following information was correct at time of going to press

Access to Communication:
Developing the basics of communication with people with severe learning difficulties through intensive interaction
Melanie Nind and David Hewitt (2004)
David Fulton Publishers

Advocacy: A review
Dorothy Atkinson (2000)
Joseph Rowntree Foundation
Pavilion Publishing

Advocacy
Your guide to advocacy
BILD and Asist
(see Resources and contacts)

Autism: Rights in Reality
This report can be downloaded from the National Autistic Society website www.nas.org.uk/content/1/c4/29/29/aaw03_ew.pdf

Away from the cameras
Simon Stevens (2003)
Community Living Page 7. Vol 16

British Journal of Learning Disabilities
– *Vol:33. No:2* June 2005
This edition focuses on information and communication.
More information from BILD
(see Resources and contacts)
or from Blackwell (Tel: 01865 778315)

Demonstrating control of decisions
by adults with learning difficulties who have high support needs.
James Edge (2001) Values into Action, for the Joseph Rowntree Foundation
Online summary at: www.jrf.org.uk/knowledge/findings/socialcare/021.asp

Donellan, A. M., Mirenda, P. L., Mesaros, R.A., Fassbender, L. L. (1984)
Analysing the communciative functions of aberrant behavior.
Journal of the Association of Persons with Severe Handicaps, 9, 201–212

Easy Guide to the Human Rights Act 1998
Implications for people with learning disabilities
Andrea Hughes and Phil Coombs (2001) BILD Publications
(see Resources and contacts)

Everyday Lives, Everyday Choices:
for people with learning disabilities and high support needs
Foundation for People with Learning Disabilities (2000)
Tel: 020 7803 1100
www.learningdisabilities.org.uk

Information for All
Getting information to people with learning disabilities
Norah Fry and RNIB (2004)
These guides can be downloaded from the library section
www.easyinfo.org.uk

Making Decisions:
Helping people who have difficulty making decisions for themselves
A series of consultation papers to help with issues of consent. Guidance for families, health professionals, social care professionals, and people with learning disabilities
Department of Constitutional Affairs
www.dca.gov.uk/family/mi/index.htm

Person to Person:
Establishing Contact and Communication with People with Profound Disabilities and those whose behaviour may be challenging
Phoebe Caldwell with Pene Stevens (1998)
Pavilion Publishing
Tel: 0870 890 1080
www.pavpub.com

Planet Advocacy
Issue:12 June 2005
Quarterly magazine produced by Action for Advocacy
Tel: 020 7820 7868
planet@actionforadvocacy.org.uk

A Practical Guide to Intensive Interaction
Melanie Nind and David Hewett (2001)
BILD Publications
(see Resources and contacts)
Rights for All – People with learning difficulties using the Human Rights Act
Values into Action
Tel: 020 7729 5436
www.viauk.org

See What I Mean
Guidelines to aid understanding of communication by people with severe and profound learning disabilities
Nicola Grove (2002)
BILD/Mencap publication
(see Resources and contacts)

Valuing People:
A new strategy for learning disability for the 21st Century
Department of Health (2001)
(see Resources and contacts)

6. Resources and contacts

The following information was correct at time of going to press

Acting Up
Multimedia profiling
Unit 304
203–213 Mare Street
London E8 3QE
Tel: 020 8533 3344
www.acting-up.org.uk

Action for Advocacy
PO Box 31856
Lorrimore Square
London SE17 3XR
Tel: 020 7820 7868
www.actionforadvocacy.org.uk

Advocating for Equality
Scope Library and Information Unit
Tel: 020 7619 7342
www.scope.org.uk/publications

'Am I making myself clear?'
Information about making your communications more accessible for people with a learning disability
Mencap
123 Golden Lane
London EC1Y 0RT
Tel: 020 7454 0454
www.mencap.org.uk

Asist Advocacy
'The Watching Brief'
Winton House
Stoke Road
Stoke-on-Trent
Staffordshire ST4 2RW
Tel: 01782 845584
www.asist.co.uk

BILD
(British Institute of Learning Disabilities)
Campion House
Green Street
Kidderminster
Worcestershire DY10 1JL
Tel: 01562 723027
www.bild.org.uk

'Challenged by Complexity'
Association for Real Change (ARC)
ARC House
Marsden Street
Chesterfield
Derbyshire S40 1JY
Tel: 01246 555043
www.arcuk.org.uk

Change Picturebank
Change
Unity Business Centre
Units 19 and 20
26 Roundhay Road
Leeds LS7 1AB
Tel: 0113 243 0202
www.changepeople.co.uk

Choice Initiative
Details of the project, training materials and video
The Foundation for People with Learning Disabilities
Sea Containers House
20 Upper Ground
London SE1 9QB
Tel: 020 7803 1100
www.learningdisabilities.org.uk

Circles Network
Person Centred Planning And Inclusion
Potford's Dam Farm
Coventry Road
Cawston
Rugby
Warwickshire CV23 9JP
Tel: 01788 816671
www.circlesnetwork.org.uk

Communication and PCP
Nicola Grove,
unpublished handout
BILD
Campion House
Green Street
Kidderminster
Worcestershire DY10 1JL
Tel: 01562 723027
www.bild.org.uk

Communication Matters
Information about augmentative and alternative communication
The ACE Centre
92 Windmill Road
Oxford OX3 7DR
Tel: 0845 456 8211
www.communicationmatters.org.uk

Communication Passports
Information about communication passports and other augmentative communication
The CALL Centre
University of Edinburgh
Paterson's Land
Holyrood Road
Edinburgh EH8 8AQ
Tel: 0131 651 6235
www.callcentrescotland.org

David Pitonyak
'Toolbox for Change' and other resources
www.dimagine.com

Department for Constitutional Affairs Human Rights Team
6th Floor
Selborne House
54 Victoria Street
London SW1E 5QW
Tel: 020 7210 1437
www.dca.gov.uk/hract

Department of Health Publications
DH Publications orderline
PO Box 777
London SE1 6XH
Tel: 0870 155 5455
Fax: 01623 724524
E-mail: dh@prolog.uk.com
www.dh.gov.uk

Disability Rights Commission
FREEPOST MID02164
Stratford-Upon-Avon
Warwickshire CV37 9BR
DRC helpline Tel: 08457 622 633
www.drc.gov.uk

Dorset People First
Total communication
2 Herringston Barn
Winterbourne Herringston
Dorchester DT2 9PU
www.dorsetpeoplefirst.co.uk/tc.htm

Foundation for People with Learning Disabilities
Sea Containers House
20 Upper Ground
London SE1 9QB
Tel: 020 7803 1100
www.learningdisabilities.org.uk

Frameworks 4 Change
Tel: 01273 204932
frameworks4change@ntlworld.com

HFT
Multimedia profiling
Merchants House
Wapping Road
Bristol BS1 4RW
Tel: 0117 9273746
www.hft.org.uk

In Control
A pilot scheme that gives people who use services greater control over their own funding budgets
www.in-control.org.uk

Information for people who have high individual support needs
Norah Fry
Tel: 0117 923 8137
www.easyinfo.org.uk

Liberator
www.liberator.co.uk

Makaton Vocabulary Development Project
offers training and resources in the use of signs and symbols
Tel: 01276 61390
www.makaton.org

Making Decisions Alliance
The Alliance campaigned for urgent new legislation on mental capacity
www.makingdecisions.org.uk

Mencap
123 Golden Lane
London EC1Y 0RT
Tel: 020 7454 0454
www.mencap.org.uk

Mental Capacity Act 2005
Including easy read summary
www.dca.gov.uk/menincap/legis.htm

Mental Health Alliance
A coalition of organisations, sharing concerns about the Government's proposals to reform the Mental Health Act (1983)
134–138 Borough High Street
London SE1 1LB
Tel: 020 7716 6782
www.mentalhealthalliance.org.uk

Multimedia profiling
Acting Up
Unit 304
203-213 Mare Street
London E8 3QE
Tel: 020 8533 3344
www.acting-up.org.uk

National Autistic Society
393 City Road
London EC1V 1NG
Tel: 020 7833 2299
www.nas.org.uk

'Notes for Parents'
David Pitonyak
www.paradigm-uk.org/pdf/Articles/notes_for_parents.pdf

Paradigm
Information on person centred planning
8 Brandon Street
Birkenhead CH41 5HN
Tel: 0870 010 4933
www.paradigm-uk.org/articlespcp.html

PoHwer Advocacy
Carol Warren House
551 Lonsdale Road
Stevenage
Hertfordshire SG1 5DZ
Tel: 01438 726990
Fax: 01438 351297
www.pohwer.net

Signalong
Training and resources
Stratford House
Waterside Court
Neptune Close
Rochester
Kent ME4 4NZ
Tel: 01634 819915.
www.signalong.org.uk

Talkback
FILO Emotional literacy project
Amersham Community Centre
Chiltern Avenue
Amersham
Buckinghamshire HP6 5AH
Tel: 01494 434448
www.talkbackamersham.co.uk

Talking Mats
can be used to help people who can understand pictures and symbols to talk about issues that are important to them
AAC Research Unit
University of Stirling
Stirling FK9 4LA
Tel: 01786 467645
www.aacscotland.com

Talking photograph albums
Plastic pockets to hold photographs and a short message can be recorded on each page
www.liberator.co.uk
www.ebay.co.uk

Values Into Action
www.viauk.org

Valuing People Support Team resources
Toolkit about advocacy
www.valuingpeople.gov.uk/AdvocacyToolkit.htm

Toolkit about involving people with high support needs
www.valuingpeople.gov.uk/IncludedHigh.htm

Widgit Software
Graphic symbols to support communication
Widgit Software
Tel: 01223 425 558
www.widgit.com